Common memories of [...] as a place at odds with the impulses of life are behind the comic and compassionate writing of these two playwrights.

Ron Blair's *The Christian Brothers* recalls a child's view of the old Catholic education system; and in it we watch, as if the theatre itself is the classroom, the funny, sad, self-revelation of a teacher who has lost faith and clings with receding vigour to a childhood glimpse of the Virgin Mary which set him on the path to his calling. It is a work which the actor Peter Carroll has made his own since 1975, travelling around Australia, to New Zealand, Canada and the United Kingdom.

A Lesson in English is Barry Oakley's tribute to a brief unhappy experience as an evening class English teacher; and in it he treats with his unerring sense of the incongruous the plight of teacher versus predatory young males, tangling with the Elizabethan courtesies of Andrew Marvell's 'To His Coy Mistress'. Blair's Brother opens his class with another example of English classic verse— a poem which perhaps reflects his own condition better than that of his students. Oakley's Stone is sunk from the start, while the Brother ends with an affirmation of ritual as the palliative to incomprehension.

Both plays pose some poignant questions about the purposes of education and the motives of its practitioners. *The Christian Brothers* is discussed in this book by Father Edmund Campion and Peter Carroll; and *A Lesson in English* by the author.

CURRENCY DOUBLE BILLS

GENERAL EDITOR: FRANK BLADWELL

The Christian Brothers and
A Lesson in English
first published in 1976 by
Currency Methuen Drama Pty Ltd.
Reprinted 1982, 1983, 1985, 1989 by
Currency Press Pty Ltd.
P.O. Box 452, Paddington,
NSW 2021, Australia

National Library of Australia card number
and ISBN 0 86819 067 5

Typeset by Queensland Type Service Pty Ltd, Brisbane

Printed by Colorcraft Ltd, Hong Kong

RON BLAIR was born in Sydney in 1942 and educated
at Christian Brothers College, Lewisham. He is a Bachelor
of Arts from the University of Sydney. He was closely
involved with the early development of the Nimrod
Street Theatre and was co-author of *Biggles*, with which
the theatre opened in 1970. In 1977 he was associate
director of the State Theatre Company of South Australia;
and in 1980 writer in residence at the Sydney Theatre
Company. He works as a free-lance writer in Sydney and
his plays include *Hamlet on Ice* and *Flash Jim Vaux* (1971),
President Wilson in Paris and *Kabul* (1973), *The Christian
Brothers* and *Owning Things* (1975), *Perfect Strangers* and
Mad, Bad and Dangerous to Know (1976), *Marx* (1978) and
Last Day in Woolloomooloo (1979).

THE CHRISTIAN BROTHERS

RON BLAIR

Peter Carroll as the Christian Brother in the Nimrod Theat production

For Don Crosby

The Christian Brothers was first performed at Nimrod Theatre, Sydney, on 1st August 1975 with:

Peter Carroll as
THE CHRISTIAN BROTHER

Setting designed by Larry Eastwood
Directed by John Bell

CHARACTER

THE CHRISTIAN BROTHER, an ageing secondary school teacher.

SETTING

A school room. At one end is a blackboard over which hangs a crucifix. At this end there is also a rostrum on which stands a teacher's lift-up desk. There is no chair on the rostrum. In the body of the classroom there is a solitary black chair. There is also, hanging on a wall about a foot over the head, a glass and wood case containing a statue of the Virgin Mary and a vase of small flowers.

The 1950s, Sydney.

A door bangs. THE CHRISTIAN BROTHER *enters wildly, a small Globite suitcase under his arm. His eyes are closed and he is chanting.*

My heart aches, and a drowsy numbness pains
My sense, as though of hemlock I had drunk—
I can't hear anyone—
Or emptied some dull opiate to the drains—
Louder, louder—
One minute past—
I can't see your lips moving—
                    and Lethe-wards had sunk—
Where's Lethe? Get out of the room—
'Tis not through envy of thy happy lot,
But—

(*His finger, which has been floating, now jabs at the chair. He looks into the far distance and takes a breath.*)

'Tis not through envy of thy happy lot,
But—
Oh come on! But ... being ... too ... happy—
Come on!
But being too happy in thine happiness—
That thou, light-winged Dryad of the trees—
What's a Dryad? (*Pause*) Come on, son. Dryad. Is it a
miracle detergent? Right.

(*He flings his suitcase on the desk, opens it and takes out a strap.*)

A Dryad, friend, is neither a miracle detergent nor
a beach towel, but a tree nymph who is born and dies
with the tree in which it lives. Heard that before?

(*He approaches the chair.*)

That thou, light-winged Dryad of the trees,
In some melodious plot
Of beechen green, and shadows numberless,

(*He straps the chair four times, beating time to the following line.*)

    Singest of summer in full-throated ease.
Now say that.

(*He closes his eyes with mock patience, trying to control the breathing his effort has cost him. He waits.*)

Thank you. Thank you for learning the poem and the meanings of the words I underlined yesterday. May I ask who wrote the poem?

(*Pause.*)

Keats will do. You don't refer to Shakespeare as William Shakespeare. If you say simply Keats I will understand. Now, since you didn't learn the poem last night what homework did you do?

(*Pause.*)

I see. Maths. And what have you told Brother Kiernan? That you spent last night learning a poem by *John* Keats? Is that what happened?

(*Pause.*)

Sly hound. And you think I'm fool enough to fall for that? Sly hound. Now listen, son, I don't want to see you put one foot—one toe!—out of step for the rest of this term. Is that understood? (*Pause.*) Right.

(*He steps back to address the rest of the class.*)

Very well, gentlemen. Consider this quotation from the *Ode to a Nightingale*:
    But here there is no light,
    Save what from heaven is with the breezes blown
    Through verdurous gloom and winding mossy ways.
Anything unusual about that? No light save what is blown?

(*Pause.*)

Well, for a start it's not very good physics, is it? When was light last blown anywhere by a breeze, eh? But then again, when did we last read Keats for his scientific opinions? No, boys, Keats is a master of the language. Listen. Think how evocative these lines are of a forest cave *redolent* with moss—write down redolent: r-e-d-o-l-e-n-t: look it up. Now listen, you just can't say these lines fast. Listen:

 With the breezes blown
 Through verdurous gloom and winding mossy
  ways.

What are you doing? What was I just saying? Well?

(*Pause.*)

And why's that?

(*Pause.*)

Answer me, you repulsive tub of lard. Stand up when you're spoken to. Eh? I'll give you "just daydreaming, sir". Put your hand out.

(*He takes his strap out of his soutane and gives the chair three of the best.*)

It's about time you woke up. Daydreaming! Life out there isn't going to be one long football game, you know.

(*Pause.*)

Come on, son, there's no need for all that. I didn't hit you that hard.

(*Pause.*)

Football won't get you through your exams. In its place it's great, but once you leave here, son, people want to see what sort of pass you've got, not how well you pass the ball.

I've seen footballers leave this school, sonny, and they thought they were Christmas. They swaggered out that front gate like their shoulders were crammed with ten pound notes. Hookers and halfbacks and wingers and props: they thought they were Christmas. Every week they were cheered to glory by the school, respected out there in the playground, photographed for the school magazine. Oh, this one was going to be a professional and that one was being feted by some Leagues Club or other. One or two of them made it—for a season or two: second grade. As for the rest, they went into the Public Service; hooked petty cash vouchers and propped up a bar. I still see some of them on old boy nights. They come back here run to fat and stare at the trophies they won for the school.

(*Pause.*)

But at least they come back. How many of you sitting here now, once you've left, will ever think of coming back and looking up your old teachers, eh? Precious few. Precious few.

(*He has walked quietly towards the chair, where he hits the back.*)

Please don't pick your nose, son. It's a disgusting habit. I remember one old boy who came back after twenty years. I showed him all the things that had happened here since his time—the new wing, the chapel, the science block. He wasn't interested. He just wanted to see this room. (*Pointing to the chair*) He had sat there. Do you know what he wanted to see most of all? That crucifix. He wanted to see if its legs were broken. He had kicked a football in the room one lunch-time and accidentally hit the crucifix. He just stood there looking up at it, at the break in the legs. The last thing left of his years at school. Then he wrote me a cheque for two hundred pounds. Conscience money, I suppose. He told me no one had ever noticed the break at the time. I said he should have got six. Do you know what he did? He put his hand out. A successful surgeon in his forties! For a minute I thought he was serious. I didn't know what to do. So I just read his cheque.

(*Pause.*)

I often wonder about him whenever I look at that crucifix. I pray for him and hope he's kept the faith. Often you see an old boy dodging you in the street and you know he's lost his faith and is too ashamed to face you. That's plain stupidity. Just remember, boys, that whatever happens to you we're always glad to see you. That's the trouble with the old boys club. You only see the successful ones. They come back here to show off their car and their clothes and their wives. You never see the ones who missed the bus. Often, they're the ones you remember. I never ask an old boy if he's kept the faith. That's none of my business. I just ask how many children he's got. That's usually the give-away. If he's got five or six, you can be pretty certain. If any of you boys should come back here as men, I won't be interested in what car you drive or how much you earn a year or how much you kick into kitty, I'll only want to know one thing: do you still practise your religion? I won't ask, mind you. It's not my business. But, boys, your faith is my business now and the Catholic faith, boys, is a marvellous gift. People out there right now are fighting to believe in something but you have the faith, given to you as a gift from birth. Hold on to it, boys, and nurture it all your lives. Some of you have seen old Brother Molloy up there on the verandah up at the Brothers' house. He's retired now and he sits there correcting papers or snoozing. But the other day, I saw him praying. Later I said to him: "Brother, what were you praying for?" And do you know what he said? (*Pointing at the chair*) You! What am I talking about?

(*Pause.*)

Right. Well, sit up properly. Where was I? Ah, yes, Brother Molloy. I said to him: "Brother, you were praying like your very soul depended on it." And he said to me: "It does. I am praying to keep my faith." To keep his faith—an old man like that!

(*A handbell rings, off.*)

Let us pray, boys, that we too will keep the faith given to us by God. In the name of the Father and of the Son and of the Holy Ghost, Amen. Hail Mary, full of grace, the Lord is with thee, blessed art thou amongst women and blessed is the fruit of thy womb, Jesus.

(*He throws a piece of chalk at the chair.*)

Holy Mary, mother of God, pray for us sinners now and at the hour of our death, Amen.

(*An electric bell rings the end of the period.*)

The French Revolution. What was the prime cause? (*Answering a hand*) Not the tennis court oath. Oh dear! Anyone else?

(*He has an array of hands to pick from. His finger wanders and points to the chair.*)

The reign of terror came after. I'll give you reign of

terror with stupid answers like that. Now think! What's a significant reason for a whole country to overthrow the certainties of tomorrow's meal. No, think! I'm not answering anything until you've had time to think.

(*Pause.*)

Reign of terror, indeed. If there's any reign of terror around here it will come from me! I'll bring down rain—from your eyes. That was a terribly stupid answer, son. I don't want to have to hit you every time you open your mouth, so keep it closed and do both of us a favour.

(*Pause.*)

Well, come on. What about sheer hunger? Isn't that worth considering? People get uneasy when there is no meal tomorrow! A hungry man is a desperate one. Hunger can do terrible things to a man. It not only weakens his body and mind: it can make him despair of the goodness of God. The only thing to be said in favour of hunger is that a starving man has no time for lust.

(*Pause.*)

A few of you could lose a bit of weight. I've noticed a growing dependence on smut in this class. This morning I saw a group of boys from this class over by the bubblers. Looking at this!

(*He produces from his desk a tame cheesecake picture from* Pix.)

The boy who brought this picture to school is no longer in this class. In fact he is no longer a member of this school. When I caught that same boy smoking last week I confiscated this.

(*He produces a cigarette lighter.*)

It seems fitting that one should destroy the other, just as that one boy if allowed to stay at this school would have as surely destroyed other boys by his polluting behaviour.

(*He lights the lighter and holds it near the pin-up.*)

But first, boys, I want you to understand that the misguided young woman who posed for this unfortunate photo has the same physical characteristics as the Blessed Virgin Mary. There is nothing intrinsically wrong with her. What is wrong is the absence of clothes and the immodest way she is disporting herself. So when you see pictures of this nature ask yourself: Would the mother of Christ be seen like this?

(*Pause.*)

Boys, the human body is a temple of the Holy Ghost and believe me, for those who abuse that temple by either posing near naked or leering on that pose are trafficking with the devil himself. And as for those who publish such photographs—in this case (*consulting the print at the bottom of the page*) Sungravure— there is a pit in hell awaiting them this very minute and in that pit is a fire (*indicating the lighter*) a world wider than this, which will rage and burn them body and soul.

(*He lights the picture, and times the burning with his stop watch.*)

That photo took exactly six seconds to burn. Gentlemen, in hell there is no such thing as time. Eternity means time without end. A million years is nothing. Absolutely nothing. Hell means torture without any end whatsoever. Think that today will end, but in hell no day ever ends and no night neither because both are one and both are without end. Is it worth risking this terrible punishment for a minute—an hour—of passing sinful pleasure? Oh, boys, it's not! So when these temptations arise, do something else. Go and play handball. Handball's great virtue is that it demands such energy that it outpaces the devil. Don't think that the Brothers don't feel these temptations of the flesh. We're human and the devil is particularly anxious that we should fall. You know, boys, don't you, that the worst punishments in hell are reserved for fallen religious? And they say that damned priests suffer terribly. That's why we play handball! You look in after school one day. You'll see a few Brothers whipping the handball. Outpacing the devil, I call it. But I personally think the best way to avoid temptation is to pray to the Blessed Virgin Mary.

(*Pause.*)

I've . . . I've actually seen the Blessed Virgin Mary.

(*Pause.*)

Take out your geography books and get on with your cross-sections.

(*He stares into space for a time, possibly still thinking about the Virgin Mary. Then he walks about the room, arms behind his back. Finally he comes up behind the chair and looks over its shoulder.*)

No, don't mind me. Just get on with your work. Just a minute—what's the idea of that? Weren't you at school yesterday? Well, didn't you listen? And look at that margin! Like a dog's hind leg. And look at this! Ink blots everywhere! The whole thing's a dog's breakfast. Heaven's sake, sonny. This work is disgusting. It's more than that. It's insulting. And it's not just insulting to me. It's insulting to God. Well, it is.

(*Pause.*)

What do those initials on the top of the page mean? Right! To the greater glory of God. And how does this squalid work glorify God? Eh? Tell me that. That's right—it doesn't. If it doesn't glorify God, who does it glorify? I'll tell you. The devil himself! He delights in filth and . . . squalor and . . . wretched margins.

(*He gives the chair four cuts with the strap.*)

You hand in work like that to the examiner next year, sonny, and you don't stand a chance. They're busy men and they haven't got time to wade through filth. Keep your handwriting clear and to the point.

(*Pause.*)

While I'm talking about exams, there's something else I should mention. Next year is of course an external exam, probably the most important you'll ever sit. One tip. Don't put A.M.D.G. or J.M.J. at the top of your page—anything that will give you away as a Catholic. And if you do a history question and you have to mention the pope, don't on any account refer to him as the holy father. That's a dead giveaway. I heard of one boy who did a lot of damage when he did the question on the unification of Italy. He said that Napoleon III was a heretic who was no doubt this minute burning in hell.

(*Pause.*)

Now that may very well be true. But a public examination with Protestant and Mason examiners is no place to say it. You're more use to God with your Leaving Certificate than back here for another year. Boys, some of those examiners are terribly bigoted people and they'd like nothing better than to make the going tough for a Catholic lad. Nothing frightens them more than to see the professions filling with Catholics. Boys and girls pouring out of the colleges and convents, and taking positions of responsibility in the professions and the Public Service . . . positions their kids aren't bright enough to win. If you have to refer to the pope—although my advice is to skip the question altogether: it's my guess it's a question put in to trap the unwary—call him: the pope. And refer to Catholics as Roman Catholics and occasionally: papists. Then they'll never guess!

(*A handbell rings.*)

Stand, please.

(*He crosses himself, joins his hands and says the Hail Mary at the end of which he crosses himself again.*)

I'm always amused at those boys who come back here a month after they've left school and call me Brother. Thirty days earlier they had been calling me "sir", as they had been for another eight or ten years before that. Out of uniform, they call me Brother—just as if they were parents. Disappointing that. Disappointing.

(*Pause.*)

A lot of old boys call me sir whether I taught them or not. It's a nice touch of respect and I like it. Some of them I taught at this very school—in this very room—before the last war. I wasn't much older than them then. We didn't worry about getting degrees much in those days. I gave those fellows their first references—much good it did some of them. You can see their names on the honour roll and the places where they fell: Africa, Greece, New Guinea. Just kids! It hits you, you know, when that happens. Blokes you got ready for maturity; blokes you taught and trained and timed. They got good passes that year and there were (*pointing to the chair*) one or two galoots!

(*Pause.*)

I remember one in particular. He was the best schoolboy five-eight I have ever seen. God, he could move! Killed in Crete.

(*Pause.*)

Take out your French books.

(*Pause.*)

He would have made the Australian team. He was a terrific bloke too. I can remember giving him his reference but I didn't know what to say. He was wild, you see—no good for an office. He looked like a dog's breakfast. No one would want him by the look of him. When he asked me for a reference I didn't know what to write. I'd never written one before, you see, so you know what I did? I copied out the one my teacher had written for me . . . word for word. Well, what did it matter? No one believes teachers' references anyway. You end up having to say nice things about some kid you wouldn't trust with the poorbox. But in this case I was pleased to do it. I had never used mine. As it turned out, he never used his. At least, I don't think the Germans asked him for it. I've still got mine though.

(*He takes out of his wallet a fragile piece of paper which has almost come apart at the folds. He reads it to himself.*)

When I look at it, I think of the old Irish Brother who wrote it, and the young bloke I cribbed it for. Both dead. I can hardly read it now, it's so faded.

(*He puts it away.*)

That's another thing you should remember about the Brothers, boys. At the State schools, after the last bell, the teachers go home to their wives and forget all about you. At the end of the week they think about their paycheck and at the end of their lives their superannuation. But boys, the Brothers give you all the time in the world. That's why I can't understand why some blokes never come back to see you. All I'd like to know is what you're doing, who you've married, and how many kids you've got—not what kind of car you drive. Some of them, of course, can't wait to get a house on the North Shore and forget you ever existed. They're the ones I never want to see. I ran into one in Macquarie Street just the other day. "Oh Brother," he says, "how nice to see you. If you ever need a check up, come and see me in BMA House or drop in to my Mosman (*Moz-man*) surgery. Ear, nose and throat." And then he ran off. Ear, nose and throat! What sort of good-bye is that? I wouldn't go and see him if I had all three dropping off!

 Right. French . . . page . . . one-one-six. Reflexive verbs. The example here is *déshabiller*, to undress. You can see in verbs like these, the . . . er . . . pronoun is used in a . . . um . . . reflexive sense, which is to say, it's inserted before the verb. (*Writing the French on the board*)

 Je me déshabille, I undress *myself:* get the idea?
 Tu te déshabilles, you undress yourself.
 Il se déshabille, he undresses himself.
 Elle se déshabille, she undresses herself.

Nous nous déshabillons, we undress ourselves.
Vous vous—

Who said that? I'll only ask once. Double homework for everyone unless the boy who said that remark owns up.

(*Pause.*)

Well, I'm not leaving here until I find out.

(*Long pause. Then he breathes out with grim satisfaction.*)

Thank you. (*Approaching the chair*) Would you mind explaining, not just to me, son, but to the whole class, what exactly it was you found so amusing about the verb to undress?

(*Pause.*)

Nothing? Oh no, I can't believe that. It must have been a gem of wit to have set these fools around you smirking. I just can't believe you said nothing. Now why not share your witticism with the whole class?

(*Pause.*)

Come on, son. I'm not going to wait all day. What was it you said?

(*Pause.*)

Nothing? Nothing! By God, sonny, don't you put me in a rage, I'm warning you.

(*The electric bell rings.*)

Stay where you are! Sit down! I'm getting to the bottom of this if it takes all day.

(*Pause.*)

Come on, son. We're waiting. You're holding us up.

(*Pause.*)

Am I to conclude, then, that your remark was a shameful one? A cheap, grubby remark which will earn the sniggers of the like-minded. Well let me tell you something, son. You have a mind like rotten cheese, with maggots crawling in it. We don't want your kind at this school. What would your mother say if she knew, eh? By God, sonny, you'd break her heart. She's worked herself to the bone for you and your brothers. She could have sat the Leaving herself three times this past ten years, she put so much into pushing you three. With the first two she had something to work on but when it comes to you, I feel sorry for her. If you spent a fraction of the time you devote to acting the fool to getting your work done instead, she might see something. You're bone idle. Why don't you wake up? Eh? Next year you're going to sit an exam and your mother won't be there to do it for you. When was the last time you passed five subjects all at once?

(*Pause.*)

The Primary Final? There's no use looking at me. I've passed my exams.

(*Pause.*)

Get out last night's homework and let me look at it.

(*Pause.*)

Eh? Don't mumble, sonny, speak up.

(*Pause.*)

So I did! I remember that now.

(*He goes to the desk and opens it.*)

I hope every boy has put his homework in this desk. If not, please do so before you leave today.

(*He takes out an exercise book. He turns the pages, all of which are blank.*)

Now let me see. Oh dear! Oh dear me! Do you call this properly done? Did your mother see this? I bet she didn't! This stuff is puerile drivel, sonny. It's insulting nonsense! Here's what I think of this.

(*He drop-kicks it across the room.*)

That's exactly what it's worth. And this is what you're worth—

(*He draws his strap and charges the chair, giving it four very strenuous cuts with the strap, speaking at the same time.*)

—with your—smart-alec remarks—and your careless, insulting, work!

(*He is finished and is trying to control his breathing while he glowers at the chair, his jaw and temple muscles working terribly. The clock chimes.*)

Stand for the Hail Mary.

(*He crosses himself and prays, muttering the prayer with his eyes clenched shut, using the time to regain normal breathing. When he has done so—it takes longer than a Hail Mary—he crosses himself again.*)

Sit down, please.

(*Pause. He looks at his watch.*)

For Christian Doctrine today, I'm going to talk about the Christian Brothers. I'm well aware that at times I'm not the best advertisement for them. (*Smiling wryly, trying to win them over*) In fact when I was a boy—I suppose the idea that I was ever a boy must surprise you. Well I was! When I was a boy the last thing I wanted to become was a Brother. A footballer, perhaps, but not a Brother. Well, here I am. And that's one of the odd things about the Brothers, boys. A lot of us never imagined we were going to be Brothers. Even the very Founder of the Order had no idea.

The man who started the Christian Brothers was, as you know, boys, a wealthy Irishman. Edmund Ignatius Rice *(writing it on the board)* came from a well-to-do family and lived in Waterford, late last century. As a wealthy merchant, Rice lacked nothing. Here was a man whose world was full of cargoes and warehouses, invoices and bills of lading. But as a man he felt . . . unfulfilled. One day he was looking out the window and he saw some kids, urchins they were, playing in the street. It struck him, really hit him, for the first time: these kids would never enjoy the advantages he'd had. He felt what can only be described as a sense of vocation. A calling. He turned to a friend who was in the room at the same time—a woman it was; Rice wasn't a pansy, you know—and he said: "I'm going to teach those kids and give them a chance. Bring them up in the knowledge and the love of God."

(Pause.)

That's how it started. And from this one man, a whole tradition began and Irishmen travelled to the United States and Australia and started up new houses. When I was a kid, most of my teachers were Irishmen. And if you think I'm tough, you should have seen them. They were ferocious! And playing football! Oh, they were amazing. I remember Brother Duffy. He was a giant. Put him in the scrum and he ran with it on his back. And fast! Give him the ball and nothing could stop him this side of the grave.

Brother Duffy. I can see him now. Running as if his immortal soul depended on it. And you wouldn't want to give him any cheek, or hand in insulting work. By jove, he knew how to use the strap.

The first year at the novitiate is where they sort you out. You can get a pretty rum lot. The first to go are the holy willies. They never last. Then they weed out . . . the unsuitables. That often takes a little longer. Too long in my opinion. At the first school I taught at there was a Brother who would have been more at home in a convent. Although from what Saint Terese of Lisieux tells us things can get pretty rugged in a convent, what with the women hurling boiling water at each other in the kitchens. Beats polishing the silver, I suppose.

(*Pause.*)

I'm glad I'm not a nun. The Christian Brothers take three vows, boys: poverty, chastity and obedience. (*Writing them on board*) You're allowed to keep a few common possessions of course—a watch or stop-watch and suchlike—but otherwise, you own nothing and earn nothing. That means no insurance policies, no mortgages, no overdrafts, no bills. It makes life a lot simpler. (*Ticking off "Poverty"*) Chastity: well, you young fellows can never understand that. But chastity's relatively easy if you're busy. (*Ticking off "Chastity"*) Obedience: that's the hard one. Sometimes you might not see eye to eye with the boss but you can't take a sicky or go on strike or demand arbitration. What he says goes and sometimes he can be pretty tough. If I'm having a hard time accepting decisions, I think of Our Blessed Lord in the Garden of Gethsemane. There, on his knees, he saw everything that was going to happen to him in the coming days: the mockery, the floggings, the crowning with thorns, that terrible journey with the cross and finally, most terrible of all, that cruellest of deaths where he alternated between gasping for breath or slumped as the nails tore through his flesh. There in the garden, days before it happened, he saw it all. In his terror he cried out to his Father not to let it happen: "Let this cup pass from me!" Don't we all say that sometimes? Why me? Why not somebody else? But Our Lord knew he had to to through with it. That's why he was born: to die in the way he did. His supernatural self knew he had to die in that terrible way. He had seen it would happen since the beginning of time. When I remember that, I accept my obligations. It makes obedience a joy!

(*He ticks off "Obedience".*)

Why do we become Brothers in the first place? We forego marriage, children, travel, the pleasures of power and ambition, friends even—it's amazing how few want to see you again after you join the Brothers. Why do we do it? Sometimes I wonder myself. If you asked them, most would say they joined to save their immortal souls. Someone once said that if Catholics had nine lives, they'd spend each one thinking about the next. But he completely missed the point. (*Producing his trump card*) We don't have nine lives! We have only one very brief one. It's on that one life, boys, that we're judged for all eternity. The soul is an immortal spirit! The Saxons, the Venerable Bede tells us, believed that life was like being at a feast in a noisy, warm and well lit banqueting hall. Outside, darkness. But Christ has revealed to us what is outside that hall—and what awaits us when we leave the banquet depends on how we have behaved. And the best way to keep the faith is to keep your mass. Keep the mass, boys, and you'll keep your faith. And remember

what Our Lord said to the rich man who asked him
the way to everlasting life: "Give up all you have and
follow me!"

Give it up! As simple and difficult as that. I want
you to think deeply about that, boys. Life is so quick
it seems yesterday that I was your age. Tomorrow I
shall be as old as Brother Molloy, correcting papers in
the sun. So! If you've got good health, and are leading
a pure life then you may well have a vocation to the
Christian Brothers. It's a wonderful vocation, boys.
Good health. You know if you've got that or not.
Think carefully about that other aspect—the sixth
commandment. Examine your conscience carefully.
Ask yourself: Have I had impure thoughts? Have I
engaged in impure talk, jokes I'd be ashamed to tell
my mother. Have I been touching myself? Hands off,
lads, hands off. Even for those of you who want to
become Brothers, there'll be temptations, boys. In a
couple of years you'll be out in the world, taking out
girls, and you'll find yourself attracted to them and
that's only natural. A word of warning. The flesh is
weak. We're only human. And if you find yourself
alone with a lass and her parents are out, well then,
boys, don't—I beg you—don't—(*with great difficulty*)
don't eat your Christmas cake before Christmas. If
you find yourself tempted by impurity, then pray.
Pray hard to the Blessed Virgin. She who has never
sinned will help you and intercede for you and obtain
special grace for you from God. Boys, never
overlook the Virgin Mary. She is a mighty powerful
lady. She was human in every way but as the mother
of Jesus she was made free of sin. And when she came
to die, rather than suffer her to be so much as tainted
by the grave, Our Lord took her body and soul off the
ground and lifted her into heaven. And if God cared
enough for her to do that, what else won't he do at

her request? You've only to ask, boys.

(*Pause.*)

I've actually seen the Blessed Virgin Mary.

(*Pause.*)

Now I don't want to see any smirks or sniggers. The first sign of a simper and that boy can leave the room.

(*Pause.*)

Of course when I told people about the vision, just after it happened, they said it was a dream. The only thing was I spoke to men of three different nationalities simultaneously, in their own languages. For about five minutes, I had the gift of tongues! I was about a year older than you, in my last year at school. I had been praying hard to the Blessed Virgin about my vocation. I wasn't sure, you see. Then one night, I'd just got into bed—the light was out—when there in the darkness at the end of my bed, she appeared. She was the most beautiful woman I have ever seen. All around her body was this light, emanating out of her in a slow, steady stream, giving off a sort of hum, like high tension cables. She was wearing a mantle of blue light and she smiled at me and nodded. I sat there for about a quarter of an hour after she'd gone and then got out of bed and went into the lounge room where my parents were entertaining an Armenian and a Chinaman. "I have just seen the Blessed Virgin Mary," I said, and both my parents, the Armenian and the Chinaman each understood me in their own language. The next day I applied for entry to the novitiate. Now that gives you some idea, boys, of the personal interest the Blessed Virgin Mary has in each and every one of us. If you think you have a vocation, then you couldn't do better than pray to her for guidance.

(*The hand bell rings. He says the Hail Mary.*)

Physics. Friction on an inclined plain. Get out your Booth and Nicol.

(*He goes to the desk, takes out his text. He sees a note in it.*)

By the way. There is dancing practice this afternoon on the tennis court from three to three thirty. Brother Farrell . . . (*After waiting for the groan to subside*) Thank you! Brother Farrell asks me to tell you that those taking the girls' parts will swop with their partners today and those who have been boys will take the girls' parts.

(*There are howls of dismay from the class—never heard by us, of course.*)

That's quite enough of that noise, thank you! It won't do you any harm to learn a few social graces. In later life you will be glad you learned to dance. And you couldn't have a better teacher than Brother Farrell. No, I mean it. The fact is . . . no, no, perhaps I shouldn't. (*Smiling at the cries of disappointment*) No, no, I'd be speaking out of turn. (*As the cries continue*) Eh? Well, I shouldn't. Not so much noise then. (*Dropping his voice*) In the thirties, Brother Farrell was the Australian ball-room champion. Apparently he was a wonder at the gipsy tap.

(*Pause.*)

Who said that? (*Advancing on the chair*) That's not funny. That's a disgusting thing to say. My God, sonny, you're a dirty hound. Put your hand out.

(*He brings the strap down on the chair three times.*)

I don't ever want to hear that sort of remark in this school ever again. And while I'm about it, there's another word I never want to hear in this school. You

all know the word so there's no need to look like that.
It should never pass the lips of a gentleman, let alone a
Catholic. A boy was heard using the word in the
playground last term and I'm sure you're perfectly
aware of what happened to him. I never want to hear
it—understood?

(*Pause.*)

It rhymes with luck.

(*Pause.*)

How many boys here are members of the Holy
Name Society? Hands up. Is your hand up or down?
(*Surveying the class*) About half the class. Not nearly
enough. I want to see the rest of you enrolled in the
Holy Name by next week. If you're not wearing
your badges I'll want to know why.

(*He looks at his watch.*)

Most of the physics period is gone already. For
homework tonight . . . (*Louder*) For homework
tonight look at those pages on friction and do the
problems on page forty-eight.

(*He looks at his watch again.*)

Next Sunday is Holy Name Sunday. Remember,
boys, never let the holy name of God ever be used
lightly and never blasphemously. God's name is
powerful and the martyrs of the early Church, often
while they were burning at the stake, found great
consolation by merely calling on the holy name of
Jesus. I would ask those members of the Holy Name
to stand and join me in singing "Holy God We Praise
Thy Name". Don't worry about the others. Stand
and we'll sing.

Holy God we praise thy name,
Lord of all we bow down before thee,
All on earth thy sceptre 'claim,
All in heaven above adore thee,
Infinite thy vast domain,
Everlasting is thy—

(*He is interrupted by a banging from behind the black-board.*)

Who did that? Eh? Brother Kiernan? Was it? What's got into him? I suppose he thinks that (*shouting at the board*) mathematics is more important than praising the holy name of God! There are some teachers here who would be better off in a State school.

(*Pause.*)

Tell me something, or better still, just put up your hands: does Brother Kiernan say the Hail Mary on the hour in his maths periods?

(*Pause. No hands appear.*)

I see. I see. Well, I'm sorry about that, boys. Maths is very important but you can be sure hell is not without its mathematicians. Boys, the really big exam is not at the end of this year or next year but at the end of our lives. A prayer to the Blessed Virgin on the hour reminds us of that and if, in his wisdom, Brother Kiernan omits the prayer on the hour when he takes you well I see no alternative than having two on the hour when I take you—or one each half hour. Whether you win a scholarship or not is immaterial. The great issue is whether or not you (*thumping out the words on his desk*) save your immortal soul! Hey! What are you doing? By God, sonny, you're a sly hound. I'm talking about your immortal soul. Do you know what that is?

(*He charges to the chair.*)

Your soul is in peril, sonny, in peril of eternal judgment.

(*He drags the chair up to the blackboard and, still holding it writes the word "soul" on the board with his free hand.*)

What's that word? Right! Soul. Do you have a soul, sonny? Sometimes I very much doubt it, you're such an animal. How do you know you have a soul?

(*Pause.*)

What? It's got nothing to do with the ten commandments! Fool of a boy! What does the catechism say? Eh? "I know I have a soul . . ." Well, repeat it after me! "I know I have a soul . . . because I am alive . . . and because I can think . . . reason and choose freely." Now take a good look at the word. And don't forget it.

(*He proceeds to beat the chair-back into the blackboard, tipping it forward off its back legs.*)

Any jokes you'd like to make? Any smart remarks? I bet you don't make smart remarks in Brother Kiernan's class. Well from now on, you're not going to make them in mine either. I've had you. I've had you right up to here. Now get outside.

(*He gives the chair a good kick, sending it flying.*)

Come on, get up, get up.

(*The chair does not move. He takes out his strap.*)

Are your going to move, son, or am I going to make you?

(*Pause.*)

Right.

(*He proceeds to thrash the chair with six cuts on the 'seat'. It will not be upright. He backs off panting, exhausted.*

By God, you're a sullen and stubborn hound.

(*Pause.*)

Come on now, out you go. Are you all right? Look at me son. Are you okay?

(*Pause.*)

There's no point sulking. Well, stay where you are.

(*Pause.*)

Look, sonny, I don't want to hit you. I don't enjoy it. It only upsets me and wastes the time of the whole class. But don't you see, you can't clown for the rest of your life. Some day or other you'll have to learn to grow up.

(*Pause.*)

Come on now. You haven't got any broken bones, have you? And I can't see any blood. So what's the fuss?

(*Pause.*)

Very well. Stay there. Don't move. Don't move an inch. If you move, sonny, I'll thrash you. Disrupting the class like this. I've a good mind to tell your mother. What would she say? Eh? (*Looking at his watch*) We should be half way through Caesar's Gallic Wars by now. (*With a hint of a promise*) Up to where he was fighting the Belgae.

(*The electric bell rings.*)

The whole afternoon's slipping away and you're responsible! All right, son. You've made your point.

If I lost my temper . . . well, I . . . I'm sorry. All right? Get up off the floor.

(*Pause.*)

My God, sonny, I trust you've no thoughts of becoming a Christian Brother. You wouldn't know what a vow of obedience was. On the other hand, a year or two in the novitiate would do you the world of good. They'd break that stiff neck. Those who can't take it soon get out, but not before they've learned something first. The soutane doesn't make the man, you know. This is merely the rag they give you. If I take it off I'm still a man and I'm still a Brother. Look. I'll show you what I mean.

(*He takes off his soutane. He is wearing a collarless shirt and black trousers held up with police and fireman braces.*)

See, I haven't got two heads. My body is arranged the same way as yours is. The big difference is, sonny, that I've learnt discipline, to accept authority. And until you've learned to accept those two things you're a spineless nothing! Now get up.

(*Pause.*)

All right. If that's the way you want to play it. I'm going to count to ten. If you're not on your feet and out that door by that time I'm going to—

(*The electric bell rings.*)

The whole day's going and we've got nothing done because of you. You're not only wasting my time but the precious time of the whole class. If you're not on your feet by the time I count ten, son, I won't be responsible for my actions. Are you going to get up? I'm going to start counting. Now's your last chance.

(*Pause.*)

I'm going to start counting in three seconds.

(*Pause.*)

One—I've started. Two. Three. I'll be absolutely merciless, son. Four. The Blessed Virgin Mary is seeing all this; how do you think she likes it? Five. Six. Not to mention your guardian angel. Seven. Eight. Last chance, son, last chance. Nine. Nine and a half. All right. Stay there. Don't move. Don't move an inch.

(*Pause.*)

Don't .think, son, that by defying me you're achieving anything. I'm not important at all. I'm just someone your parents have asked to teach you a few things before you start earning your own living. And to tell you the truth, son, I can't teach you much. Sometimes—sometimes I wonder why I'm here at all. Getting myself into a state. I can't educate you, son, only life can do that and a really educated man is a dead one. All I do is give you an undercoat, a primer, and then a first coat to be going on with. Defiance isn't a bad thing sometimes. The martyrs had it. By and large, it's not a bad thing for a young bloke to have, defiance. But boys, remember Luther. Defiance can end badly. If it makes heroes, it's also the maker of damned men. Remember Martin Luther; be careful who you defy. The Church is a bad enemy to have, boys. And those of you who are thinking of becoming Brothers and priests, pray hard. Remember that it's not a way of ducking responsibility. I remember one fellow—years ago now—he loved football and he thought that life as a Brother would be one long series of games. His teachers flattered him and they treated him well and they made him a prefect and asked him to eat with them from time to time. He played handball with them after school and at Christmas he visited them at their holiday place down the South Coast. He saw them as they were: beer drinkers, card players, intrepid surfers. They assumed he would be soon one of them. So did he. Why not? No nagging wife or income tax or insurance policies. He could go on playing football.

They told him to pray and he did. He prayed hard to the Blessed Virgin. Then one night—and you don't have to believe me: even the Church doesn't ask you to believe in the miracles God has wrought—one night, this boy saw, actually saw the Blessed Virgin Mary. He told me she was the most beautiful woman he had ever seen. All round her body was this . . . this light and it was streaming out of her, giving off a sort of hum like the sound you hear from high tension cables. She smiled at him and for a short time this boy found he had the gift of tongues—that he could speak in several languages which were identified as Cantonese and a dialect of Armenian. Boys, that man, sustained by his vision, became a Brother and when I run into him, as I do from time to time, I ask him if what he saw all those years ago has helped him through the years. He says . . . he doesn't really know. At the time, they dismissed his vision. He now wonders whether or not it was some self-induced miasma or adolescent mirage. He says he often wonders what it might be like with a wife and a mortgage. "Then leave," I tell him. "You're not too old to begin! Nobody wants you to stay here if you're not happy." He says its only the devil tempting him with doubts and that he must pray; for, he says, there's nothing more comic than an old man who is both broke and looking for a wife. "That's pride," I tell him, "and that's the devil talking if ever I heard it. Pray, I say to him, and he says he does. He says if only he could see *her* again. He doesn't want to talk in tongues or anything like that. But just to see her one more time: to see the light streaming out of her body. Just once. Then all his doubts and terrors would be gone and he would be young again.

(*The electric bell rings—a long time.*)

I tell him he'll have to wait for the grave.

(*He goes to the chair and lifts it up gently.*)

Come on, son. You won't learn anything down there. You've done nothing all day. You're just wasting your parents' money and my time. There's nothing I can do for you. You're on your own now.

(*He puts on his soutane.*)

You've done nothing but skylark and muck about ever since you came to this school. The other Brothers feel the same. You're just a nuisance. I understand your parents want you to become a doctor. Is that right? Well, let me tell you something, son. At the rate you're going the nearest you'll get to a doctor is retreading his tyres. I don't know what to do with you. There's no point hitting you. I'm sick to death of hitting you. There must be some way of educating you . . . some technique.

(*The hand bell goes.*)

Before you break for dancing class—(*Raising his voice*) Could I have a little less noise, please.

(*Pause.*)

Thank you. Before you break for dancing class, may I remind you that today is the feast day of Blessed

Oliver Plunkett, bishop and martyr. On this day three hundred years ago, Bishop Plunkett was hanged by the English at Tyburn and after his death, which he met without fear or anguish, his body was taken to Germany and his head to Rome. The torso has since been brought back to England, where it now rests at Downside Abbey, and his head has been returned to Ireland and is in Armagh Cathedral. Let us pray we too will keep the faith with the same devotion and courage as did Bishop Plunkett in the face of English torture three hundred years ago. Stand for the litany, please. In the name of the Father and of the Son and of the Holy Ghost, Amen,

Lord have mercy. Christ have mercy. Lord have mercy.

Christ hear us. Christ graciously hear us.

God the Father in heaven	have mercy on us
God the Son, redeemer of the world	have mercy on us
God the Holy Ghost	have mercy on us
Holy Trinity, One God	have mercy on us
Holy Mary	pray for us
Holy mother of God	pray for us
Holy virgin of virgins	pray for us
Mother of Christ	pray for us
Mother of divine grace	pray for us
Mother most pure	pray for us
Mother most chaste	pray for us

(*He goes to the desk, takes out a tin of paint, opens it, stirs it, and as the litany proceeds, paints the chair blue.*)

Mother inviolate	pray for us
Mother undefiled	pray for us
Mother most amiable	pray for us
Mother most admirable	pray for us
Mother of good counsel	pray for us

Mother of our Creator	pray for us
Mother of our Saviour	pray for us
Virgin most prudent	pray for us
Virgin most venerable	pray for us
Virgin most powerful	pray for us
Virgin most merciful	pray for us
Virgin most faithful	pray for us
Mirror of justice	pray for us
Seat of wisdom	pray for us
Cause of our joy	pray for us
Spiritual vessel	pray for us
Vessel of honour	pray for us
Singular vessel of devotion	pray for us
Mystical rose	pray for us
Tower of David	pray for us
Tower of ivory	pray for us
House of gold	pray for us

(*The lights fade to blackout.*)

END OF PLAY

INTIMATIONS OF IMMORTALITY

EDMUND CAMPION

In the mid 1950s, the time of Ron Blair's *The Christian Brothers*, most Australian Catholic boys and girls were being educated in Catholic schools.

The schools were ricketty, unpainted, crowded buildings that had to be paid for from the Catholics' own pockets. They were staffed by over-worked and under-prepared men and women like Ron Blair's character, who made up for their lack of polish by rare self-sacrifice and love of their pupils. The pupils came for the most part from working-class extended families and at school absorbed a culture most of them would never lose. *Litany*, *novena*, *contrition*, *purpose of amendment*, *genuflection*—the special language of the culture would turn up in their speech for the rest of their lives, whether or not they *lapsed* or still *practised*.

At the same time, other Australian boys and girls were reciting each week at School Assembly:

> I love my country, the British Empire.
> I salute her flag, the Union Jack.
> I honour her King, King George The Sixth.
> I promise cheerfully to obey her laws.

Catholic schools did not go in for that sort of mysticism. They had their own hymnody. Each Friday before lunch the whole school would be marched over to the parish church for Benediction of the Most Blessed Sacrament. How readily it comes back into memory: the guttering candles on the high altar, the sweet smell of incense afloat, the flaming majesty of the priest robed in gorgeous cope and surplice, the reedy singing of the *O Salutaris* and the *Tantum Ergo*, the gabbled *Divine Praises* flung back in unison towards the priest's head, the numinous and faintly terrible white disc in the golden monstrance presiding over a packed church . . .

and afterwards the somehow sanctified, no longer
everyday, peanut butter sandwiches and water from the
bubblers.

If it were their turn, the junior classes at Friday's
Benediction might sing a popular hymn:

> I am a little Catholic,
> I love my Holy Faith;
> I will be true to Holy Church,
> And steadfast until death.
>
> I shun the schools of those who seek
> To snare poor Catholic youth;
> No Church I own—no schools I know,
> But those that teach the truth.

Rarely more than two verses. Older classes would scorn
such kid stuff; and their hymn would be the rollicking

> Full in the panting heart of Rome,
> Beneath the Apostle's crowning dome,
> From pilgrims' lips that kiss the ground
> Breathes in all tongues one only sound:
> God bless our Pope, the great, the good!
> God bless our Pope, the great, the good!

In those days you rarely experienced Mass during school
hours, because the ancient rules of the Church required
you to fast from food and drink after midnight before
receiving Holy Communion. In the mid 1950s, these
rules were relaxed and daytime Masses became normal.
But Ron Blair's pupils would have been trained as old-
time Mass servers, or *altar boys* as we called them. As
youngsters in the school they would have learned to
make the responses to the priest in Latin . . . quickly, the
way most priests said Mass. They would have known
the agony of being wakened for early morning Mass,
hurrying down the cold street before breakfast, thumb-
ing the sleep from their eyes. Perhaps too some of them
would remember the shame of dropping the heavy

Missal when changing it from one side of the altar to the other; or else the hairy experience of tripping over the sanctuary bell and sending it rolling down the altar steps; or even the horror of getting the giggles while *on the altar*.

They would certainly know the peculiar moral casuistry attached to the fasting laws: if you went to sleep with chewing gum in your mouth and then swallowed it, was the fast broken? did toothpaste break the fast? how did one compute midnight—summer time? metropolitan time? eastern standard time?

Weighty questions. The Church law of not eating meat on Fridays gave other questions. Was it a sin to eat Vegemite sandwiches on Friday? beef broth? Bonox? And again, when did Friday start and finish? Sex too was heavy with questions for the casuist. As much as Judaism, Catholicism was a religion of law.

It was also a religion of certainty. The smallest child learned to rattle off the Green Catechism:

Q. Who made the world?

A. God made the world.

Q. Who is God?

A. God is the Creator of heaven and earth and of all things and the Supreme Lord of all.

Q. How do we know that there is a God?

A. We know that there is a God by the things that He made.

In higher classes, students would ponder the subtleties of theology, using Archbishop Sheehan's *Apologetics and Christian Doctrine* for textbook, a crowded work that fashioned the logic-chopping of the medieval School-men to an Australian accent and whose argumentative-ness may account for the high incidence of Catholics amongst Australian lawyers and philosophers.

Apart from law and theology there were religious practices to be encouraged in the school. Passing a church, one tipped one's hat; some, mostly girls, even made the sign of the cross. In the street, one always greeted a priest or brother or nun. Grace was said before meals; and if you were eating in a restaurant you made sure you blessed yourself first, to show you weren't ashamed of being known as a Catholic. Of course, you might already be known as such, since you were wearing the black and white badge of the Holy Name Society for men and boys. Your elder brother in National Service camp was exhorted by "A Rat of Tobruk" in his pamphlet *So You're Going Into Camp* to proclaim his faith by saying morning prayers each day on his knees. On the walls at home there would be cheap Italianate pictures of Jesus and the saints, who were spoken about conversationally as if they were absent members of a large family, distant rich uncles or aunts. In some homes everyone knelt round the table after tea and recited the Rosary of the Blessed Virgin Mary. In such small ways the unseen realities of a faith and its peculiarities were brought close to young Australians.

Their parents knew that the faith made them different from other Australians. After the Second World War they had seen, in the countries of Eastern Europe, the leaders of their faith systematically picked off and silenced. The internationalism of their religion made Australian Catholics feel personally this Soviet persecution. They responded by setting up a secret mass movement to oppose Communism in Australia. *The Movement*, as it was called, remained secret until the end of 1954. Since then, much has been written about it and its leaders; but the foot-slogging activism of its rank and file has gone unremarked. These are the fathers and mothers of Ron Blair's school.

The extraordinary sacrificing of time and energy was something bred into them by their school system. To build those schools and keep them open, the Catholic working class had to scrape every penny from its own resources. Every one of them believed that the community should help support their schools; and every one of them resented with a sullen, deep, unnoticed anger the refusal of the community to help. They did not enjoy the alienation of being second-class citizens.

It went with being Irish; for most of the Australian Catholics were Irish. The Irish knew that life was tough and you had to make the best you could of it. So they built schools where their Catholic and Irish identity could be preserved and where their children could be given the chances denied themselves. Irishmen had once been the schoolmasters of Europe. And although the English conquerors stole their land and killed their priests and closed their schools, the Irish never lost their respect for book-learning. At the lowest, it could help a labourer's son get into the Public Service, as Ron Blair's Christian Brother knew.

It all went together: Catholicism, Irishry, and getting ahead in a hostile world. Opening the first of the new Christian Brothers' schools in New South Wales in 1887, Brother H. B. O'Hagan said that their main aim would be to see that the boys adhered to "the faith of their fathers". That day they probably sang the Irish tribal chant (one cannot call it a hymn) which Ron Blair's schoolboys also would roar gustily:

Faith of our fathers, living still
In spite of dungeon, fire, and sword:
Oh, how our hearts beat high with joy
Whene'er we hear that glorious word!
Faith of our fathers! Holy Faith!
We will be true to thee till death.

Our fathers, chained in prisons dark,
Were still in heart and conscience free:

How sweet would be their children's fate,
If they, like them, could die for thee!
Faith of our fathers! Holy Faith!
We will be true to thee till death.

EMOTIONAL MEMORY
PETER CARROLL

When I first read Ron Blair's script I knew at once that I
could understand the character and play it. It was an
intense feeling of identification with the man and his
situation. This is a feeling which happens very in-
frequently to an actor but when it does the excitement is
enormous because it means that one's acting springs
spontaneously from within and does not have to be
methodically applied from external sources.

I was educated by the Marist Brothers in the 50s so
that I felt I knew the kind of education system that Ron
Blair was writing about. I have also been a teacher
(albeit in State schools) both in Sydney and in the UK,
so that I could identify with the pressures of teaching
and the attitudes which are often forced upon teachers
because they are the kind of authority figures against
which the pupils need to rebel.

There can be great differences between the image one
has of teachers when at school, and their "real"
personalities. Having met several of my own teachers
after I left school, I felt a mixture of disappointment and
relief to realise that they were not so terrifying, so
eccentric or so confident as I had remembered them. It
was rather unnerving to discover that they were likeable
people, just like you and me, who had problems and
frustrations and failures as well as successes. The Brother
is, of course, seen only in the classroom, and his
personality emerges only as clearly as a child's eye will
let it. If there is exaggeration, it is the exaggeration in
which every pupil likes to indulge.

The education system which is portrayed is no
longer with us in such an extreme form. But although
some aspects of it might be considered brutal by today's
standards I did not think so when I was being taught. I

was aware that the Brothers were motivated by a desire to serve God by teaching pupils and if that involved physical punishment then it was usually given without malice.

Schoolday experiences are so potent. Working on this play has caused me to relate many of my own experiences and to listen to many amazing stories from acquaintances. They are always compounded of amazement ("Do you know what he did?"), frustration ("We used to have to do that *four* times a week!"), bravado ("So I said that I wouldn't do it and his face went *blue*!"), bitterness, affection and a whole jumble of emotions which are both exciting and distressing to recall. It is, however, Ron's achievement that his play manages to be so much more than just a series of very funny school stories.

As an actor I may neither judge my character nor sentimentalise him. What others would call faults are only his way of reacting to a difficult situation. He became a Christian Brother because he thought he had a vision of the Virgin and now so many years later when he begins to doubt that experience he has only his need to help the pupils to sustain him, and the remnants of an outmoded teaching technique.

The language of the play is complex, exact and startlingly truthful to the rhythms of the classroom. The structure of the play is also precise and clear. Each night, playing it, I was aware of how beautifully shaped it was and how precisely it moved. It is a play which documents among other things the attitudes and language of the education system of the 50s which has produced my generation. So I feel a very close identification with both the matter and the manner.

The play is very exciting to act. I have not felt such *intense* contact with an audience before. The contact was immediate and prolonged. Both the laughter and the silences were the result of a very intimate sense of recognition. An actor is able to feel truth rather than to analyse it, and it *felt* right.

It is a very fine play and one which is, I think, actor-proof. Nevertheless, I was the first to play it and for that privilege and exciting experience I am eternally grateful.

* * *

It was at John Bell's suggestion that I first joined the Nimrod Theatre and he was also the director of this particular play. For both these decisions I owe him more than I can repay. Once again, with this play, he had the courage and insight to present an unperformed script, and so give us a better understanding of our society. I do not think that I could have handled the play without his guidance. His direction is always demanding, concerned principally with peeling away any extraneous actions until it is "right". This involves doing each section as many ways as possible. His attention is both to the play and to the actor who is performing in it. He pays the actor the great compliment of being unstinting (and accurate) in his praise and criticism. John is also a product of the Marist Brothers, and so we shared a frame of reference which enabled us to work quickly. I am glad of this opportunity to thank John publicly for his continued encouragement, support and inspiration. Australian theatre owes him a great debt.

COMMENT

(Some excerpts from press reviews of the first season of *The Christian Brothers* presented at the Nimrod Theatre, Sydney, as a double bill with *Mates* by Peter Kenna.)

Romola Costantino, *Sydney Morning Herald* 6th August 1975:

The Christian Brothers might offend certain Roman Catholics, although I do not think it is intended to do so . . .

Peter Carroll . . . finds complete fulfilment in the role of the elderly teaching Brother addressing his unseen class. It is an acting tour-de-force, in which he holds the stage for over an hour.

The voice, the gestures, the expressions, all echo memories hidden since schoolboy years. But Mr Carroll, and the author, have a deep understanding of what goes into the person of a teacher who seems at times a tyrant, a bully, a weakling, a cajoler, a threatener and then suddenly a friend, a confider, at times still an innocent, and at times a worn-out, desperate man.

The Brother's class—his "bo-oys!"—may see him as a figure of hate; some of the audience saw him as a figure of fun. But I don't think Mr Blair and Mr Carroll are so simple; the Brother is a very human, struggling figure, and Mr Carroll modulates to a mood of tender beauty as he utters, alone without his class, the gentle cadences of the litany to himself.

Judy Barbour, *Nation Review* 8th-14th August 1975:

It's cliche now that the concept of mateship in Australian folk history has a submerged homoerotic element. The merit of the Blair-Kenna treatment is that it dramatises this proposition so that what has become commonplace in social theory gets a new look. In the first play the Brother . . . recalls with wistful nostalgia the glow of comradeship when he was taken up as a schoolboy by the Brothers and found to have a vocation. From within this circle of male camaraderie, the timid man looks out at the female, awesome as the mother of God, horrifying as the mate of men . . .

Director John Bell has brought out the nerve and strength of the two men in skirts who dominate the performance, and has subtly played them off against each other in a way that goes quite beyond superficial judgements of priestly celibacy and transvestism as brothers under the skin.

Brian Hoad, *The Bulletin*, 16th August 1975:

Goodness knows what (*Mates*) has got to do with Ron Blair's new monologue for a Christian Brother which starts off the evening. Guilt perhaps. And no doubt the Brothers have done their bit to screw up the libido of a nation. But if Kenna had wanted to draw that thread into the picture, he, as one of the Brothers' victims, was well qualified to do so. A longer drag show extending to the cut-off point of vacuous boredom followed by *Mates* would have been sufficient and a more courageous approach to a prickly piece of theatre.

Kevon Kemp, *National Times*, 18th–23rd August 1975:

The Christian Brothers is a very funny piece, even though many of its laughs are unashamedly sectarian, borrowing too many of the old Orangemen and Masonic anti-Roman cliches.

As a fading Christian Brother teacher of the old beat-it-into-them style (still current, according to one or two lads I spoke with in the audience) Mr Peter Carroll gives a one-man show of some brilliance . . .

In the writing Mr Blair has given the teaching Catholic Brother enough roundness to suggest the earnest stupidity that lies under the priest's poor technique as a pedagogue. Here and there, towards the end of the play, Mr Blair seems to relent a little of his hardness, giving a miserly pinch of Mr Chips savour to Mr Carroll's character—but it is a little sour. Mr Blair clearly cannot gloss over all the beltings so vigorously applied to, luckily, an imaginary pupil . . .

I suspect the experience may be releasing for many who look back, with some rue, on a Catholic childhood.

Geraldine Pascall, *The Australian*, 22nd August 1975:

As the ageing, chalky Brother, whipping his class with his ever ready strap as well as his intolerance, rigidity and frustrations, Carroll immerses himself in a characterisation that gnaws at all the flailing Brother's mental and physical habits and attitudes.

It is a play written for a lot of immediate laughs, but with an underlying bitterness—and even a sympathy made possible by time—that seems to yell of the remembered horrors of an impoverished, sectarian education.

BARRY OAKLEY was born in Melbourne in 1931 and educated at the Christian Brothers College, St Kilda, and the University of Melbourne. His plays were among the first performed at La Mama theatre in the late 1960s and he was an early member of the Australia Performing Group. He now works in Sydney as a free-lance writer. In 1977 he was writer in residence at the University of W.A. and at Monash University in 1978. He has published three novels and a volume of short stories. His published plays include: *From the Desk of Eugene Flockhart* (1966), *Witzenhausen Where Are You?* and *A Lesson in English* (1967), *The Feet of Daniel Mannix* (1971), *Beware of Imitations* (1973), *Bedfellows* (1975), *Scanlan* and *The Ship's Whistle* (1978), *Marsupials* (1979), *The Great God Mogadon* (1980) and *Politics* (1981).

A
LESSON IN
ENGLISH
BARRY OAKLEY

All I want is a little kindness and understanding! *Cartoon by Les Such reproduced by kind permission of the New South Wales Teachers' Federation.*

A Lesson in English was first performed at the La Mama Theatre, Melbourne, on 6th July 1969 with the following cast:

STONE	Martin Phelan
REMAINING	Paul Bailey
CAST	Graeme Blundell
	Meg Clancy
	Bethany Lee
	Rod Moore
	Kim O'Leary
	Margo Smith

Directed by Geoff Milne

CHARACTERS

STONE, a teacher
GRANT, the tallest student
TWO INSPECTORS
STUDENTS, seventeen and eighteen year olds, about
  fifteen in all, of whom ten have speaking roles.

SETTING

A classroom. The STUDENTS sit at curved tiered
seats, half facing the audience.

STUDENTS *come in. They get out books, talk noisily. As the minutes pass and the teacher still does not appear they get more and more boisterous, shouting, throwing books. They get worse, transistors are turned on, feet make a drumming noise—the combination eventually producing a distinctive throbbing sound; then the door is thrown open: enter* STONE, *a plainly dressed schoolmaster in his middle thirties.*

STONE: Stop, stop! Quiet, d'you hear? I've never heard anything like it—never! What are you—animals? Nothing but brute beasts? I'm ashamed, ashamed! Why are you here, why? Ever asked yourselves that? Wasting your parents' money, your teachers' time—it's a disgrace, an absolute disgrace! Look at you—your clothes, your radios—spoilt, pampered, everything you want! People in developing countries clamouring for knowledge—not you, oh no. You take it all for granted. All you want to do is pick up your diplomas and get out—make money, buy yourself a car, get yourself a girl—kicks—you're in it for kicks . . . What's in it for me? What's in it for number one? Parties, records, booze—well, it's not your fault. We're the ones who have failed, the older generation. We're the ones supposed to pass on the good things, the true and the beautiful—but what do you do—the music, the art, the literature—just turn on your transistors . . . I look around and I despair, d'you know that? *These* are the people we're giving a higher education to. If they're like this, the leaders, then what of the others? We're doomed, I tell you—doomed, finished! We'll fold up one day—you, me, all of us, western civilization, the lot—we'll fold up like a great big zeppelin, we'll collapse with a crack—and to the sound of the

Rolling Stones and crashing Coca Cola bottles we'll fall—and it's a long way down to the ground!

(*Silence. Trembling a little from his outburst*, STONE *goes to the rostrum and calls the roll. They all answer, save* GRANT.)

Grant? Grant? Are you here Grant, or are you not?

(GRANT *is deep in a magazine. Finally he registers.*)

GRANT: Sir!

STONE: Bring down whatever it is you're reading, Grant.

(*They titter.*)

Come on, come on, bring it down. Give it to me. Yes, you can all laugh. We all know about this magazine, don't we. *Playboy*. Hot and blue from the States. Look at it. Aren't you ashamed?

GRANT: No sir, I enjoy it, sir. It's good fun in my estimation, sir.

STONE: Yes, you enjoy it. Good fun. A section on sports cars, the right things to wear, what to drink, what to think—and lo and behold in the midst of all this innocent enjoyment what do we find? The *Playboy* sex-kitten of the month. You shouldn't read this magazine, Grant—you should study it.

GRANT: I do, sir. I do study it. Very closely indeed.

STONE: You misunderstand me, Grant. You should study it—objectively. For what it is. Do you know what *Playboy* is, class? A piece of merchandise. Glossy sex, in a slick package. You peel back the skins, work your way hungrily through the outer layers like a peeping Tom parting the curtains, and there's the lovely forbidden fruit—the *Playboy* Bunny. All pink and provocative. She unfolds with the page, she seems to rise out of the magazine into your arms. It costs you a dollar, but you pay it. It's smart. It's the thing to do . . . Sex isn't private any more, isn't decent any more—isn't personal, isn't *sacred* any more. Sex is a coin in the slot machine . . . And *girls*—listen to me. Don't be surprised when the stranger comes at you from the dark of the lane. Don't blame the mugger who slips his hand over your mouth. Blame yourselves. Blame your own empty-headed sex for agreeing to pose for pictures like this!

(*He unfolds the picture, holds it up, tears it methodically into bits, then hands the magazine back.*)

GRANT: Oh gee, Mr Stone. That didn't belong to me. You shouldn't have done that. It's not mine. Arthur Blake collects those pictures.

STONE: Well you tell Arthur Blake I'm very sorry, but you shouldn't have brought that filth into class . . . and now, let's get started.

(*He unrolls a large sheet of paper, and hangs it up prominently. On it, in letters as large as possible, the poem* To His Coy Mistress *is printed.*)

Open your poetry books at page seventy-one. It's most appropriate, you know—because we're going to look at the whole business of love this afternoon. Yes. But in a civilised, humane way. The way an educated person regards it—not as something sneaky and cheap, oh no. Something fine and good. Page seventy-one. *To His Coy Mistress* by Andrew Marvell. Oh, by the way. Two weeks ago I set you an essay on *Macbeth*. So far I have had two essays handed in to me. Two. Let me remind you that, should you fail to complete the stipulated number of essays for the year, failure is automatic. But perhaps that doesn't worry you. Let me also remind you that the inspectors from the Department are in the building. Moving through the rooms. Looking at people's work. Checking, assessing, evaluating the position. Should they honour us with their presence this afternoon, I trust you'll give of your best . . . well now. Andrew Marvell. He's called a metaphysical poet. Anyone tell me what metaphysical means?

(*Long pause.*)

Hmm. I thought not. You're pragmatists, the whole lot of you. Hedonists to a man. Utilitarians. You find philosophy as dull and incomprehensible as chastity. Let us analyse the word. Meta is Greek for after or beyond. Now, Armstrong—metaphysical.

ARMSTRONG: Beyond—beyond the physical, sir.

STONE: Clever, Armstrong, clever. Beyond the physical, eh? Is such a phrase intelligible to you? Looking at your bulk, I doubt it.

ARMSTRONG: Beyond the physical—it means—the spiritual.

STONE: Good, Armstrong. An idea has struck you. Pause now, and let the novelty wear off. Yes. The spiritual. Beyond the reach of the physical sciences. The sphere of philosophy. And so Mr Andrew Marvell is called metaphysical—he didn't just *experience* the emotion of love—he *thought* about it. When does it say the poem was written, Cohen?

COHEN: In the 1650s, sir.

STONE: Right. And who was running England at this time?

COHEN: The Commonwealth, sir. Cromwell. After the Roundheads beat the Cavaliers in the Civil War. They caught King Charles and they tried him and they led him to the block and chopped off his head. Very grave and dignified he was. And after they beheaded him many of them were afraid about what they'd done and so Oliver Cromwell—

STONE: That'll be enough thank you, Cohen. The Civil War was a metaphysical war rather than a political one. This is often forgotten. Cromwell was more interested in the Kingdom of God on Earth than constitutional issues. And Marvell was a Cromwell man, though he lived to regret it. But enough. Let us look at the poem, the poem. Class, this is a memorable moment—the moment when we advance to the murmuring shore, as it were, of genius. When we stand before literature in all its majesty. Ah yes. When I, the traveller, bring you, the new generation, to the forgotten city. I am the intermediary, the teacher, the man with a foot in both worlds. In this confrontation, class, there is drama. We will read four lines each, starting with you, Elizabeth, and proceeding round the class. Ready?

ELIZABETH:
Had we but World enough, and Time,
This coyness Lady were no crime.
We would sit down, and think which way
To walk, and pass our long Love's Day.

BARBARA:
Thou by the Indian Ganges' side
Shouldst Rubies find: I by the Tide
Of Humber would complain. I would
Love you ten years before the Flood:

STONE: Yes, yes, come on—oh, it's Grant. It's always

Grant. Tell me, Grant, what is it? Four times a week, whenever I take you for English, the war of attrition goes on. Maybe you tap a pencil. Or kick your feet. Or whisper and mumble. Snigger and nudge. You never let up. You don't like me, do you, Grant? You think I'm put here purely to torment you. And all we do is drive one another mad. Read your lines, if you would.

GRANT: (*in a flat monotone*)
>And you should if you please refuse
>Till the Conversion of the Jews.
>My vegetable Love should grow
>Vaster than Empires, and more slow.

STONE: Terrible. About as romantic as a cattle truck. Let's have some feeling—Judy.

(*An attractive girl reads the next lines.*)

JUDY:
>An hundred years should go to praise
>Thine Eyes, and on thy Forehead Gaze.
>Two hundred to adore each Breast:
>But thirty thousand to the rest.

(*The noise breaks out again, a spontaneous single force, of transistors, roaring, and drumming feet as at the beginning of the play.*)

STONE: Stop that! Stop it, do you hear? You growl and rumble like animals. I won't tolerate those stockyard noises! Read on please, Schultz.

SCHULTZ:
>An Age at least to every part,
>And the last Age should show your Heart.
>For Lady you deserve this State;
>Nor would I love at lower rate.

VERONICA:
>   But at my back I alwaies hear
>   Time's winged Charriot hurrying near
>   And yonder all before us lye
>   Desarts of vast Eternity.

GARRY:
>   Thy Beauty shall no more be found;
>   Nor, in thy marble Vault, shall sound
>   My ecchoing Song: then Worms shall try
>   That long preserv'd Virginity:

(*The noise erupts again.*)

STONE: My God, I've had just about enough of it! Never in all my teaching experience have I had to put up with a performance like this. It's disgusting, d'you hear? Disgusting! All right. Just wait. Yes, I've got a pretty fair idea who's at the bottom of it. Just wait. I'll catch that person. You'll see, my fine fellow. Oh yes. This beautiful poem! A thing of beauty! A joy for ever! You profane it with your stamping hooves, you beasts! Read on.

GWENDA:
>   And your quaint Honour turn to dust;
>   And into ashes all my Lust.
>   The Grave's a fine and private place,
>   But none I think do there embrace.

STONE: There now! Why can't you all read it like that? Beautifully spoken. I give praise, mark you, where praise is due. Next.

BILL:
>   Now therefore, while the youthful hue
>   Sits on thy skin like morning dew—

STONE: Mumble, mumble, mumble. You're mangling it, Reeves. I can't bear to hear it. I'll finish the poem myself. Listen:

> And while thy willing Soul transpires
> At every pore with instant Fires,
> Now let us sport us while we may;
> And now, like am'rous birds of prey,
> Rather at once our Time devour,
> Than languish in his slow-chapt pow'r.
> Let us roll all our Strength, and all
> Our sweetness, up into one Ball:
> And tear our Pleasures with rough strife,
> Through the Iron gates of Life.
> Thus, though we cannot make our Sun
> Stand still, yet we will make him run.

Great words, class. Great words. I am moved, as you see. I blow my nose unashamedly. True metaphysical wit, classical grace. Poetry that is adventurous in thought, yet subdued to the texture of the verse— producing an effect at once contemplative and exciting, gravely formal yet mysteriously suggestive. I could go on and on. Would that the inspectors were here, I might almost say, at this moment, to witness it. With his manipulation of the images of exaggeration—make a note, make a note—he shows not only a truly serious sense of sprightly wit, but also, in its threefold movement—the strophe, antistrophe and epode of Horace, mark you—a sense of form which provides a wholly new dimension. Have you got that? It's rather good, though I say it myself.

(*He pauses while they scribble, wandering the floor in pride.*)

I wax quite eloquent when the spirit is moved . . . Well now. Let us look a little closer. M'yes. To use the phraseology of our times, let us see if you—dig it.

We'll see. First, the overall theme—what is it—Fletcher?

FLETCHER: He wants—he wants—his girl—to—to come across with it.

(*The noise again.*)

STONE: That will do, you animals! Must I get a stockwhip? The poet wants his mistress—the word had a slightly different connotation in those days, mark you—he wants his mistress to—er—he is, er, advocating that they enjoy their love now—why? Judy?

JUDY: Because she's beautiful, they're young, and age will soon come.

STONE: Excellent. That's the theme, class. Enjoy love now, he's saying—tomorrow may be too late. Make a note. Now let us see how this theme is worked out, eh? What precisely is Marvell saying in the first quatrain, Armstrong?

ARMSTRONG: The first what, sir?

STONE: A quatrain. Not some form of locomotive, Armstrong—merely the first four lines, my boy.

ARMSTRONG: He's saying that if they had plenty of time, it wouldn't matter so much. But they haven't much time, they're in a hurry.

STONE: Why, Armstrong? Why haven't they time?

ARMSTRONG: Maybe he's only got a few minutes and he wants—he wants—to do it quick and lively.

(*The noise.*)

STONE: Shut up! Stop! Enough! Are you in rut like the beasts of the field? On heat, like the bitches in the streets? That awful noise! That mad drumming of the blood! The leer of swinish instinct, the bray of the herd! I can't stand it, I won't have it, do you hear! Punishment! I'm punishing you all for this, get that clear! Keeping you in after classes, yes, every man jack of you. I'll report the matter to the principal, if there's a repetition! He'll have something to say about it, mark my words. Sometimes it's a matter of deep regret that the strap and the cane are no longer in use. When I was your age, the teachers laid about them with a will—thick and fast. Still, there are ways and means. Ah yes. Don't think for one single moment you're getting away with this. I address my remarks to the ringleaders in particular—and well I know who they are—other instructors wouldn't wait a moment longer—they'd haul them out here and now— holus bolus—but I'll bide my time—cool my heels—till the real culprit shows his hand. I know his little game. He's conniving, conspiring—call it what you will—he's plotting to get me. He's got it into his empty little head that I'm his enemy. He harbours a grudge. Will stop at nothing to unseat me from my position. All right, up there. I accept your little challenge. Eagerly. With alacrity. I know who you are. The gloves are off now. A naked clash of wills. A battle for power. The dialectic of friend Hegel. Thesis, antithesis, synthesis. We'll see, we'll see . . . Armstrong, it's not that he's only got twenty minutes. Not that at all, do you hear? Mr Marvell is not in the back seat of some bomb at the drive-in, which seems about the limit of your imagination. He's talking about time as such, as Judy pointed out, time *qua* time as the scholastics would have it, *tempus fugit*, the nature of time—that nothing is firm, nothing is solid, all slips away. Think of it, you young pagans. All—all slips away! The transistor batteries go flat! The chrome on the fender rusts! That's life's confidence trick on you all! Ha ha! Your real punishment! Yes! Ha ha! Make a note! Ha!

(*He leans limp against the rostrum, exhausted but triumphant. A short pause.*)

And now, and now he elaborates the thought—

> Thou by the Indian Ganges' side
> Shouldst Rubies find: I by the Tide
> Of Humber would complain. I would
> Love you ten years before the Flood:
> And you should if you please refuse
> Till the Conversion of the Jews.

What is the point of this elaboration? No answer, eh? I thought as much. We must do some spadework, I fear. Background—that's what you need. Background. By now one would expect you to have it. But no—not these days. History and geography are old hat these days. In my time, we had to learn the length of every river, the heights of the mountains, the dates of the battles. Not now. Ask me. Ask me the length of a river. Any river. Go on. Ask!

ELIZABETH: The Nile, sir.

STONE: In all its windings the Nile measures no less than 4,145 miles.

BARBARA: The Amazon.

STONE: 3,900 miles from the basin to the sea. What a river!

VERONICA: The Murray.

STONE: 1,600 miles—not much, but it's the best we can offer in the antipodes.

GARRY: The Irrawaddy.

STONE: Ah—1,300 miles. And navigable for large steamers along 900 of them. See? That's education. It gives you background. Confidence. Bearing. The information may not be immediately useful, of course. But the discipline is there. Knowledge *qua* knowledge. For its own sake. The liberal ideal. Prepare to take notes. (*Dictating*) The Ganges: a great river of Northern India, formed by drainage of the southern Himalayas. It rises in the Garhwal State and its lower course focusses the river system of Bengal, in whose bay it falls after a course of 1,500 miles. The Humber: an estuary on the east coast of England, formed by the rivers Trent and Ouse. The Flood (your history, too, is weak, weak): a reference to the story in Genesis six to nine of God's anger at the iniquity of mankind, whom He therefore proposed to destroy by a deluge—note that, you inhabitants of the cities of the plain! Rubies: The most valued of all gemstones. A red transparent variety of crystallised alumina. There. That's better. You've *learned* something. We progress at last. Now, to the poem.

> My vegetable Love should grow
> Vaster than Empires, and more slow.

Why vegetable, Maxwell? Why vegetable love?

MAXWELL: I—I—don't know, sir.

STONE: Wait—wait. There was a whisper—a stage whisper—*sotto voce*—I heard it—it came from up there. Stand up the student who whispered that remark.

GRANT: What remark sir?

STONE: Yes, Grant. It's you I suspect for all your air of injured innocence. You hope to trap me into repeating the allusion. Something about roots.

(*The noises resume briefly.*)

Stop that—a dirty and disgusting remark. I'm asking the student responsible—I demand that he come forward like a man. Grant?

GRANT: That's hardly fair, sir. You're just assuming it was me.

STONE: I have grounds, Grant, I have grounds. Have you not spent the bulk of your school year in devising subtle ways to make my life miserable?

GRANT: No, sir. You've got the wrong man, sir.

STONE: I'll be the judge of that. I want no more nonsense from you, get that clear. What is vegetable about his love, Grant?

GRANT: He means it could grow slowly, sir, if there was time.

STONE: Correct, Grant. You can be acute, if you wish. You can even be pleasant. Let us pinpoint the poet's metaphor in rather more careful terms—the inspectors—should they honour us with a visit—will then be able to see that adequate information is being imparted to you. Vegetable—take this down—could mean having the power of sense perception as well as being like a plant. (*Speaking at mounting speed*) The anticlimax is gained by the contrast between the size of the love and the time it takes to grow.

(*Slight suggestion of the noise.*)

Stop that—that'll do, do you hear—and rhythmically this is conveyed in the verse by the sudden pause in the middle of the second line and the three heavy monosyllables (*pointing to them on chart*) emphasised by the long drawn out vowels. In other words, the reader taking vegetable in the old Latin sense would meet a sudden reversal of meaning. The poet proceeds:

> Two hundred to adore each Breast
> But thirty thousand to the rest.

(*The noise again: powerful.*)

Aaargh! That damned roar! Sewer rats! Pigs! I'll teach you!

(*Seizing a wooden pointer he rushes round madly, shouting curses, hammering and belabouring them as they crouch over their benches in self defence.*)

Pff! Huh—the meaning—huh—of that little—huh—couplet, I take it from your performance, is only too obvious. So we move on—I'm tired, you know—I'm weary of this—sick at heart of the whole business of chalk and talk and the Hegelian clash of wills—we move on to part two of the blessed thing (*mumbling half to himself*) damn fool of a poem. In part one, we find the thought most wittily elaborated, as I have indicated. However, part two sounds something of a jarring note. All would be well, this dallying between lovers (*slight noise*)—please—all would be well, I say, were it not for the fact that, and I quote—

> At my back I alwaies hear
> Time's winged Charriot hurrying near
> And yonder all before us lye
> Desarts of vast Eternity.

Class, does not this render perfectly the feeling of desolation, the sense of betrayal, that comes with the thought of death? What epigrammatic force! What a reflection on the horrors of the tomb! Make a note of that.

(As they scribble, he slumps down in the chair, dejected and weary. Unnoticed, the shortest of the students (not GRANT) races out, gets up on a stool, and pins a Playboy *Bunny over the chart of the poem.)*

Deserts of vast eternity. Think of it, class. Mankind, in short, condemned to be kept in after school—forever. You're too young, of course. Death means nothing to you, I know, any more than hunger or thirst or loneliness. We belong to the anaesthetised generation. Let us proceed. (*Noticing the nude, strangely subdued*) Ah—hold—wait, wait. What's this I see? While I sat there and pondered, while I pleaded on your behalf, you pin up your golden calf. A naked woman. Not Abraham's bosom and the vision of our fathers—but the thirty-six inch bust. I demand—to—know who perpetrated that outrage. I want to know who pinned up the pin-up. This is my day—ah yes. The coy smile on the face of that naked carnivore tells me that. You've declared war today, I know it. Snipe at me from your prepared positions. Hurl your grenades. Overturn the forces of law and order. Well, I feel proud, even elated. Yes, you bring me to life. Because even here, in this mean shabby classroom on the outer borders of civilised life, the great historical forces pulse on—through us. Let us resume! Let us commence the age old struggle anew! Let us do battle for leadership of the tribe in obedience to our atavistic urges! (*Ripping it down, tearing it up*) My second *Playboy* Bunny in half an hour. You pull down what we hold as precious, and I do the same for you. That picture was pinned at a considerable height. I want all the boys to come out in turn and reach with their right arm to that point.

(They file out. Only GRANT, the tallest, reaches the spot comfortably.)

Ah. I thought so. Caught you. My arch-enemy, the ringleader of the forces of evil, the rebel angel. What are you going to offer me, Grant? All the *Playboy* Bunnies of this world, if only I will bow down and acknowledge you? Well, I won't. I propose to defeat you, to punish you for your acts. For perhaps the first time in so senior a class, I propose to resort to the strap. Grant, stand over there and await your punishment. Armstrong, go to the principal's office and fetch the senior strap.

(ARMSTRONG *exits*.)

GRANT: I didn't do it. You can't prove that I did it. Stop picking on me. You strap me, and you'll be sorry. I'll tell 'em, I'm warning you—I'll tell 'em the lot.

STONE: Oho, you threaten me, do you? I'll double your punishment for that. Do you deny you did it?

GRANT: I deny it. Someone got up on that stool.

STONE: Who? You don't answer? If you didn't do it, you put someone else up to it. It's all the same. I know you hate me. Strap them that hate you, give lines to those that persecute you. That's my policy.

(ARMSTRONG *returns with the strap, an enormous affair with handle and tassels*.)

Hold out your hand, Grant.

GRANT: I'm warning you. I'll pay you back for this.

STONE: Out with your hand, out. You're enjoying this as much as I, I know that. You love to play the martyred hero. To be the big boy before the herd. Well, you've lost! lost! lost!—the other hand—lost! lost! lost!

(GRANT *reels, collapses in pain, passes out.*)

God, that was good. Exhilarating. Makes the teacher's job worthwhile. Leave him there. On we go, ever forward, over the shattered bodies of the rebellious, the enemies of right reason—forward, ever forward! Meanwhile, back at the ranch. Let us return to that monumental bore, fop and turncoat, Andrew Marvell.

> Thy Beauty shall no more be found;
> Nor, in thy marble Vault, shall sound
> My ecchoing Song: then Worms shall try
> That long preserv'd Virginity:
> And your quaint Honour turn to dust;
> And into ashes all my Lust.

(*The noise breaks out, loud, uncontrollable, menacing. He tries to stop it, but it proceeds, then pauses of its own accord.*)

Ah yes, have your say. I knew that was coming. But I'll batten it down, I'll beat it back into the black holds of your libidos, you ravening wolves. I'll harness you, you dogs, and crack the whip—

(*It starts again. Seizing the strap, he runs at them shouting a battle cry, and lashes at them again and again, but the noise only gets worse and all the male students hold up Playboy nudes. At the height of the battle, the door opens, and two official-looking men enter without speaking. The noise stops at once and everyone, STONE included, freezes as if suddenly petrified.*)

STUDENT: The inspectors!

FIRST INSPECTOR: Resume your seats. Mr Stone, return to the rostrum. You and you, revive that student.

STONE: Welcome, gentlemen. You choose, as always, the psychological moment. We were in the middle of a keen debate on the nature of—love. As you see, many students have contributed opinions. (*Collecting the* Playboy *girls from desks and floor*) One—two—three—four—five—six. Six opinions, and interesting ones they are too.

FIRST INSPECTOR: Mr Stone, we have no alternative but to hold an enquiry into these regrettable incidents. At once. Here and now.

STONE: You regret them, do you, gentlemen? So do I, so do I. Let us all try to enquire and regret these incidents out of existence. Let us neutralise them with an official report.

FIRST INSPECTOR: Kindly resume your place at the rostrum. We propose to question the boy. Immediately. While his memory is fresh.

SECOND INSPECTOR: You are—treating a poem, I see. It is a—poetry lesson that we interrupted. I want the rest of you to proceed with an essay, and not be distracted by our proceedings. You will write three hundred words on the following topic: Marvell, like Milton, was a Puritan poet and also a Christian humanist. He illustrates the dilemma of a sensitive and serious temperament caught up in a civil conflict which he deplored. Discuss. Answers will be collected at the end of the lesson. Proceed at once.

FIRST INSPECTOR: Boy, what is your name?

GRANT: James Alexander Grant, sir.

FIRST INSPECTOR: You have been punished, it would seem. What was the reason?

GRANT: Mr Stone accused me of pinning up a *Playboy*

Bunny while his back was turned.

SECOND INSPECTOR: You deny that you did it?

GRANT: I didn't do it, I swear it.

SECOND INSPECTOR: Mr Stone, your back was turned?

STONE: I wasn't watching. I was thinking, contemplating—praying that they'd be spared the anger of the Lord. An ungrateful and pampered generation. May the Lord have mercy on them.

SECOND INSPECTOR: You weren't watching. You didn't see the culprit?

STONE: No. But I have evidence. Strong evidence. He is the only boy tall enough to reach to the height the photo was pinned. I tested it.

FIRST INSPECTOR: What's your answer, Grant? Speak up, boy.

GRANT: The stool. Someone got on the stool. I have fifteen witnesses to prove it.

FIRST INSPECTOR: Class, without mentioning any names, was the stool used?

CLASS: (*chanting in unison*) The stool! The stool! The stool! The stool!

FIRST INSPECTOR: Enough! It seems evident that you may have punished the wrong person, Mr Stone. That would seem to be the inference, on first examination.

STONE: It seems nothing of the kind. This student's been conducting a campaign against me. He bears (*shouting back at the class*) a grudge! A grudge! A grudge!

GRANT: You're the one who bears a grudge. All last year I could do nothing wrong. I was your "buddy", your "bosom pal"—yes, that's what he used to call me. Until one night—

STONE: Silence! You're dragging in personal matters! Violating confidences!

SECOND INSPECTOR: Let the boy speak. He has a right to be heard. A classroom should be fair and democratic. Speak up, lad.

GRANT: Last year Mr Stone was very friendly with me. I did jobs for him—got his sandwiches for him, ran messages. We were in the same boarding-house at the time. He took me for drives in his car, we went swimming and fishing together, he gave me presents—

STONE: Silence! I gave you presents! And look what I get in return! A fine friend! Is there no gratitude?

SECOND INSPECTOR: Stop interrupting! What led to the termination of this relationship?

STONE: Relationship! Order, order in the court. I protest! Is there no judge to whom I can appeal? There was no "relationship". I was new to the town at the time, I hadn't had a chance to make friends, so I let this boy—let him, you understand?—at his request—become friendly. I *permitted* him to accompany me on various outings, I *suffered* him to be present.

GRANT: Suffered? You asked me—even ordered me. And if your command wasn't obeyed, you'd plead!

STONE: Plead? I never, never pleaded. A teacher pleading with a student? Never. There was no relationship save that of friendship. I took the boy up.

He was alone, his parents lived twenty miles out on a farm, he was raw and crass and lonely—and I took him up. I drove him to the city, I took him to art galleries, the museums, the theatre. I treated him like a son—*educated* him!

GRANT: Yes, you educated me. I learned a lot, I learned more in that year than I've ever learned before. And it wasn't book-learning either.

STONE: Oh, you Machiavel! Ingrate! These are the very lies you've been spreading about me all these months behind my back! Making me into some kind of Fagin, a corrupter of youth! Rumours! Lies! You spread them around—in a town that lives on scandal and gossip! How the evil little shopkeepers gobbled it up!

GRANT: You deserved it, it was your own fault. You taught me too much. Those parties in your room, with kids you picked up in the pub—

STONE: Lies! Lies! We discussed poetry, art, theatre—

GRANT: And that slide evening in your room—just you and I—lies too?

STONE: Ah, you make it sound evil and twisted. You were the evil one, behind that smooth angel's face. Consider my position. I had come from the city, to this raw country town—as cold and remote as Vladivostok— I was deserted, I was alone—I needed something—someone—anyone—to hold on to against the provincial cold, the provincial barrenness. And then I met James Alexander Grant. He was polite, intelligent, eager to learn. He was proof that something could flower in this barren soil. I marvelled!

GRANT: You marvelled—and you invited me to your room.

STONE: Let me finish. Let me tell you. O silent inquisitors in your gunmetal suits—I had been on a trip. A trip to Japan. He knew I had slides. He kept pestering me to see them. So I showed them to him. But not all. There was one in particular I would not show him. Never, never, never . . . The show was over, I was out in the kitchen making coffee. I came back. He had this slide in the projector, he'd found it—I'd only brought it back from Japan as a joke, you understand, an awful kind of souvenir, a grotesque curio, a warning even, to the pleasure loving youth of our times—

GRANT: It was awful, unbelievable, a man and two women—and as he came into the room he crossed its path—it fell on him—it was grey-coloured as if he had slime on his shirt. He stopped with this dirty picture all over him, and I saw him for what he was. He stood there in the light of it, it was on his face and his arms. And I went out, I left the room, and never spoke to him again. He begged me not to tell anyone—and I didn't, I haven't, until now.

FIRST INSPECTOR: Mr Stone, kindly report to the principal's office at the end of the lesson. And make sure those essays are collected. Good afternoon.

STONE: A good afternoon—a wonderful, exhilarating afternoon. One we will all remember, gentlemen.

(*They go out.*)

Stop writing. Put down your pens. Now I can teach you something. Perhaps the most useful lesson of your life. About the nature of things. About our lot, our fate. We are all—listen! listen to me!—we are all double beings, creatures bisected, amphibians. Do you understand? In public, in the clear light of the classroom, I've tried to instil correct behaviour, discipline, what is good and true—then I too go home to my room! We all have our two faces, the public and the private. Every day we make the transition, we cross from one to the other. I'm no hypocrite! I'm human, like everyone else. All of us act out the same charade—every day we make the transatlantic crossing! This is our fate. Learn this from me—my first, my last, my one true lesson! Rational animals, that's what we are. Driven by urges. Driven to be admired, to be loved, to be kind, to be cruel, greedy, noble, brutish—man! The currents throb through, driving us in every direction! Learn this—that we're here to suffer, and you've graduated. To write essays in suffering, to pass with honours in pain! Round and round we go, day in, day out, cramped in our capsules, rooms, cars, beds—waiting for the time when the hatch blows off, and we float alone in the night! Save us, you women! Relent and take us in!

(*As he finishes, he holds up a nude, then pins it over the poem, and they all read the final lines in unison.*)

ALL:
> Now let us sport us while we may;
> And now, like am'rous birds of prey,
> Rather at once our Time devour,
> Than languish in his slow-chapt pow'r.
> Let us roll all our Strength, and all
> Our sweetness, up into one Ball:
> And tear our Pleasures with rough strife,
> Thorough the Iron gates of Life.
> Thus, though we cannot make our Sun
> Stand still, yet we will make him run.

(*A brief pause.*)

STONE: Come on, what's the matter with you? Make the noise. I order you to make the noise! Tap the feet! Clear the throat! Let the transistors sound!

(*The noise starts, slowly, gets steadily louder and louder; he beams, approves, conducts it like a symphony, urging them on. Then the bell goes for the end of class, and with a quick sweep of his pointer he brings it to a halt. Lights out.*)

END OF PLAY

THE SALMON YEARS

BARRY OAKLEY

School: a miniature society, a micro-Gulag, with supreme leader, teacher-lieutenants, and other ranks (the kids). A society far more regimented than our everyday one: you may have to wear special clothes, sit in a certain place at a certain time, share a desk with someone unpleasant, stand up when you're told, call people Sir.

As well as being a regimentation, school is also an intensification: the classroom is a public place, somewhere between courthouse and theatre. If you shine or suffer humiliation, you do it before a crowd. Forty of your peers see you blush, hear you stutter, or enjoy the teacher's contempt for your ignorance ("No, Oakley, everyone did not have feuds in the feudal system; out with your hand").

If you were strapped and cried, if you fainted (as I did during a lesson on compound fractures) or worst of all vomited (poor Kevin Langley, doomed to have his lunch on his own from then on) your humiliation was absolute. Weaklings and sissies were only allowed to wander the peripheries of the herd.

As well as being a ritual ordeal, school was also a quest for the holy Certificate. On! To the next chapter, to harder and harder vocabs, to the analysis of impossibly baroque periods from Gibbon, to the cabbalas of cosines, Fibonacci numbers, surds. Endless salmon years of swimming against the current, up rapids increasingly steep till one reached the headwaters, where the final sorting and judging were done.

That was school for me, when I was a student. Then, when I became a teacher myself, I found I was a victim still. The order that I had endured at the Christian

Brothers did not extend to country technical schools. Each day, each class, was a battle. Daily I confronted writhing monsters, Hydras with forty heads, whose restlessness could only be stilled temporarily with stories, performances. Then, bored or rebellious, the ominous swaying and wriggling would start again.

I found myself in a position of power, but almost impotent. I found myself in a situation of knowledge (fresh from the university, the bearer of culture, transmitter of the received wisdom) but almost totally ignorant of the world. I seemed an authority figure, but had none—the headmaster, remote and aloof, kept it in his office.

I was trapped between a rarified literary culture and an earthy popular one, between reason and instinct, and that, I came to realise, was the teacher's essential role—the scapegoat. The teacher's fate is to represent and manifest the curriculum, the established order of knowledge and relationships, to the raw and the untutored—he is a missionary, a bearer of the tidings to wild tribes, in constant danger of being found wanting by his superiors and boring by his congregation. And the penalty, in each case, is some kind of death.

If we define politeness as the refusal to acknowledge embarrassing truths, then the curriculum is a form of politeness. But on the curriculum there may be literary works that are not forms of politeness. In *A Lesson in English* the luckless Stone flails his class for their indifference to Marvell, but his desiccated pedantries have a reverse effect, and only succeed in releasing their sexuality, in response to the feeling at the heart of Marvell's poem.

They speak to each other (class and teacher) across an enormous gulf, and it takes an awareness of the strength and frailty of sexuality (in the life of Stone, in the life of the students, and in the life of the poem) to bridge it. At the end of the play the remarkable distance between blackboard and desk has closed, and Stone and his students are one.

As to productions of the play, it is the second that springs most to mind. It was done in a small and draughty theatre over a garage in Carlton. In my innocence I had invited along some of my friends. What awaited me was a humiliation rivalling that of Stone himself.

Rain banged down on the tin roof, the lead actor did not know his lines, and the ensemble work of the class suggested that they had been selected at random off the street. The chill wind cutting across the audience's legs from the side door was as nothing compared to the frigid spectacle up on the boards and I spent most of the time with my head down, waiting for the anarchy to end.

After the charade, I was led, a condemned man, to an area divided off by a torn drape. The green room. Sherries were served by a man in a dinner suit, and the wake began. I was asked to speak, but would not. Two old ladies who had come all the way from Ballarat asked me to sign their programmes. Like the production, it was theatrical in the worst sense, and I remember stumbling down the stairs afterwards vowing never to write another play.